SEA LIFE

Colour By Number

Book by Sachin Sachdeva (Author/Illustrator)

1=Dark Orange   2=Light Orange   3=Light Brown   4=Dark Green
5=Blue   6=Light Blue   7=Pink   8=Dark Red

1=Dark Grey   2=Light Grey   3=Light Brown   4=Dark Brown

5=Dark Green   6=Blue   7=Pink   8=Dark Red

1=Dark Grey   2=Light Grey   3=Light Brown   4=Dark Brown

5=Blue   6=Dark Green   7=Purple   8=Dark Purple

1=Dark Pink   2=Light Pink   3=Blue   4=Light Blue

5=Light Brown   6=Dark Grey   7= Dark Green   8=Light Grey

1=Light Brown 2=Purple 3=Light Purple 4=Yellow
5=Dark Red 6=Light Blue 7=Blue 8=Pink

1=Dark Grey   2=Light Grey   3=Light Brown   4=Blue

5=Yellow   6=Dark Green   7=Light Green

1=Tan Brown   2=Light Tan Brown   3=Dark Red   4=Pink

5=Light Brown   6=Dark Brown   7=Blue   8=Dark Green

1=Light Brown 2=Dark Brown 3=Blue   4=Yellow
5=Pink   6=Dark Green   7=Dark Orange 8=Light Orange

1=Blue   2=Light Brown   3=Light Blue   4=Dark Grey
5=Light Grey   6=Dark Green   7=Dark Purple   8=Light purple

1=Pink   2=Light Brown   3=Dark Green   4=Yellow

5=Purple   6=Blue

1=Blue   2=Light Brown   3=Red   4=Dark Red

5=Dark Green

1=Red   2=Dark Red   3=Pink   4=Light Brown

5=Dark Green   6=Dark Brown   7=Yellow   8=Blue

1=Light Blue   2=Blue   3=Light Brown   4=Pink

5=Light Green 6=Dark Brown 7=Light Grey

1=Yellow   2=Orange   3=Light Brown   4=Light Grey

5=Dark Grey   6=Dark Green   7=Blue   8=Light Purple

1=Dark Grey   2=Light Grey   3=Light Brown   4=Dark Brown
5=Dark Green   6=Red   7=Yellow   8=Blue

1=Blue   2=Light Brown   3=Dark Green   4=Dark Red

5=Light Pink 6=Yellow   7=Light Grey   8=Dark Grey

1=Red   2=Light brown   3=Dark Green   4=Yellow

5=Blue   6=Dark Red   7=Pink   8=Dark Yellow

1=Red   2=Yellow   3=Light Green   4=Blue

5=Light Blue   6=Dark Brown   7=Dark Grey   8=light Grey

1=Dark Grey   2=Light Grey   3=Light Blue   4=Blue

1=Black   2=White   3=Dark Orange   4=Light Grey

5=Light Blue   6=Blue

You might like few other Colour by Number books
which are available on Amazon. Do check them out!!
I am giving few bonus pages from "BUTTERFLY" book.
Hope you enjoy coloring them too!

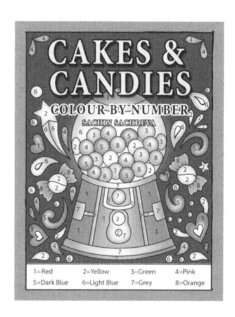

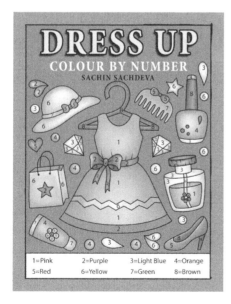

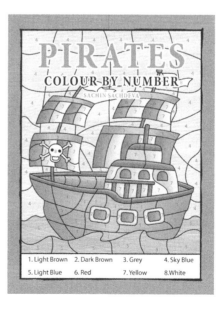

1= Yellow   2=Brown   3=Blue   4= Green

5=Pink   6=Purple   7=Red   8=Orange

1= Yellow   2=Orange   3=Blue   4= Green

5=Pink   6=Purple   7=Red

1= Yellow   2=Brown   3=Blue   4= Green

5=Pink   6=Purple   7=Red   8=Orange

Thank you for purchasing the book. I hope you or your family member enjoyed coloring the pages.

Being a self-published author and illustrator, it's very difficult to reach out to people or spend lots of money on paid marketing. My sales rely on buyers feedback and their satisfaction which motivates me to create more quality content for people of all ages especially children.

Kindly **leave ratings and feedback** on Amazon so that it will help other people in deciding to purchase my books. I'll be very thankful to you.

If you want to write any personal note, feel free to send email at **sachdev.sachin15@gmail.com**

I respond to all the emails I receive.

Thank you
Sachin Sachdeva
Author and Illustrator

Made in the USA
Coppell, TX
31 October 2019